FINGERPICKING Yuletide

ISBN 0-634-08198-5

Visit Hal Leonard Online at www.halleonard.com

HAL•LEONARD®
CORPORATION
7777 W. BLUEMOUND RD. P.O. BOX 13819 MILWAUKEE, WI 53213

INTRODUCTION TO FINGERSTYLE GUITAR

Fingerstyle (a.k.a. fingerpicking) is a guitar technique that means you literally pick the strings with your right-hand fingers and thumb. This contrasts with the conventional technique of strumming and playing single notes with a pick (a.k.a. flatpicking). For fingerpicking, you can use any type of guitar: acoustic steel-string, nylon-string classical, or electric.

THE RIGHT HAND

The most common right-hand position is shown here.

Use a high wrist; arch your palm as if you were holding a ping-pong ball. Keep the thumb outside and away from the fingers, and let the fingers do the work rather than lifting your whole hand.

The thumb generally plucks the bottom strings with downstrokes on the left side of the thumb and thumbnail. The other fingers pluck the higher strings using upstrokes with the fleshy tip of the fingers and fingernails. The thumb and fingers should pluck one string per stroke and not brush over several strings.

Another picking option you may choose to use is called hybrid picking (a.k.a. plectrum-style fingerpicking). Here, the pick is usually held between the thumb and first finger, and the three remaining fingers are assigned to pluck the higher strings.

THE LEFT HAND

The left-hand fingers are numbered 1 through 4.

Be sure to keep your fingers arched, with each joint bent; if they flatten out across the strings, they will deaden the sound when you fingerpick. As a general rule, let the strings ring as long as possible when playing fingerstyle.

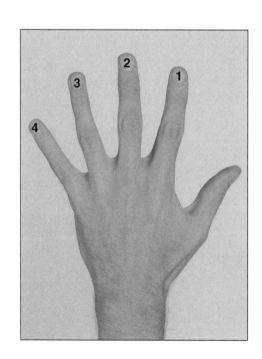

The Christmas Song
(Chestnuts Roasting on an Open Fire)

Music and Lyric by Mel Torme and Robert Wells

Drop D tuning:
(low to high) D-A-D-G-B-E

Verse
Slowly

*Barre 3rd finger

help   to   make   the   sea - son   bright.   Tin - y   tots   with   their   eyes   all   a - glow   will

find   it   hard   to   sleep   to - night.   They   know   that   San -   ta's   on   his   way.   He's load - ed

lots   of   toys   and   good - ies   on   his   sleigh.   And   ev - 'ry   moth - er's   child ___   is   gon - na

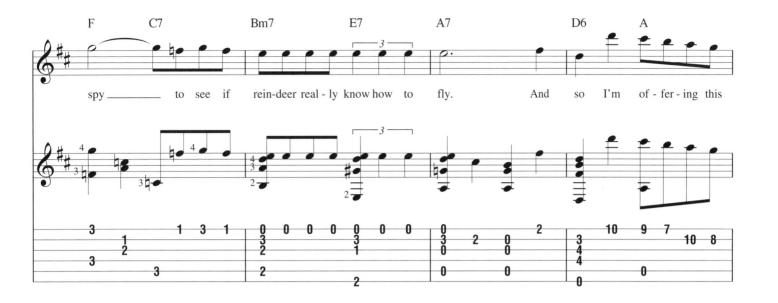

spy _____ to see if rein-deer real - ly know how to fly. And so I'm of - fer - ing this

sim - ple phrase to kids from one to nine - ty - two. Al - though it's been said man - y

times, man - y ways, "Mer - ry Christ - mas to you."

Blue Christmas

Words and Music by Billy Hayes and Jay Johnson

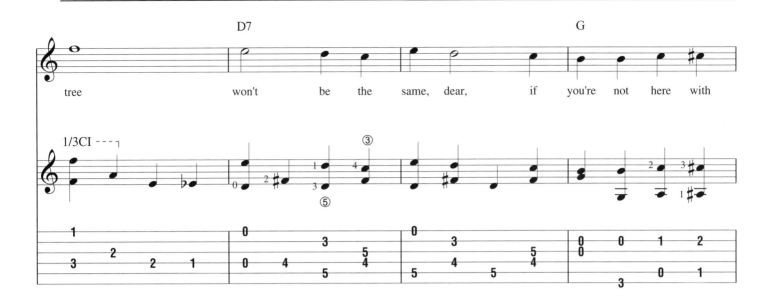

tree won't be the same, dear, if you're not here with

me. 2. And when the Christ - mas of white, but

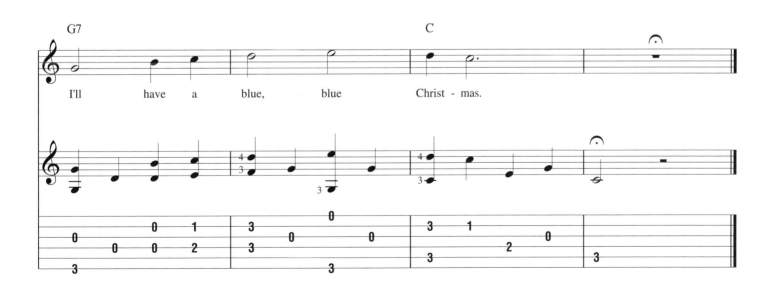

I'll have a blue, blue Christ - mas.

Do You Hear What I Hear

Words and Music by Noel Regney and Gloria Shayne

do you see what I see? _____ A star, a star,
do you hear what I hear? _____ A song, a song,
do you know what I know? _____ A Child, a Child

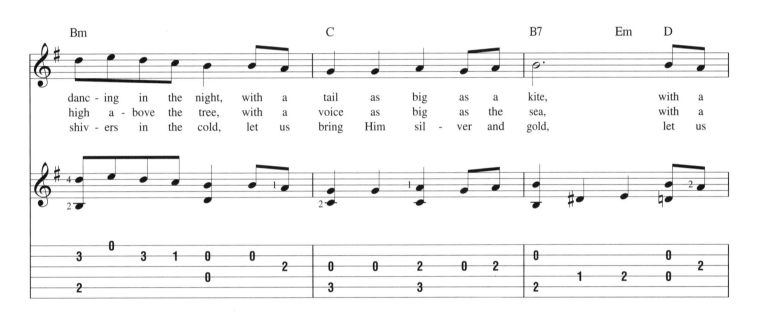

danc - ing in the night, with a tail as big as a kite, with a
high a - bove the tree, with a voice as big as the sea, with a
shiv - ers in the cold, let us bring Him sil - ver and gold, let us

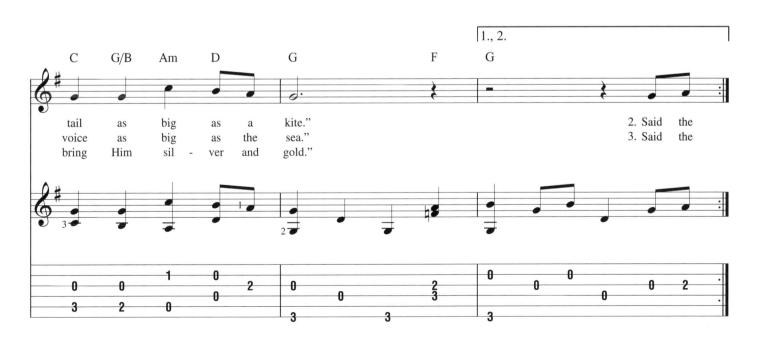

tail as big as a kite."
voice as big as the sea." 2. Said the
bring Him sil - ver and gold." 3. Said the

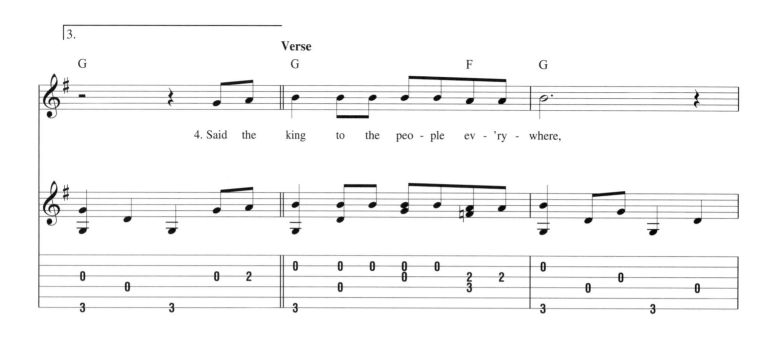

4. Said the king to the peo - ple ev - 'ry - where,

"Lis - ten to what I say! _____ Pray for peace, peo - ple ev - 'ry -

where, lis - ten to what I say! _____ The

Child, the Child, sleep - ing in the night, He will bring us good - ness and

light, He will bring us good - ness and

light." _____

Frosty the Snow Man

Words and Music by Steve Nelson and Jack Rollins

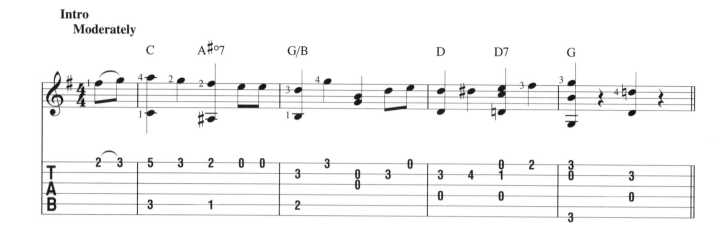

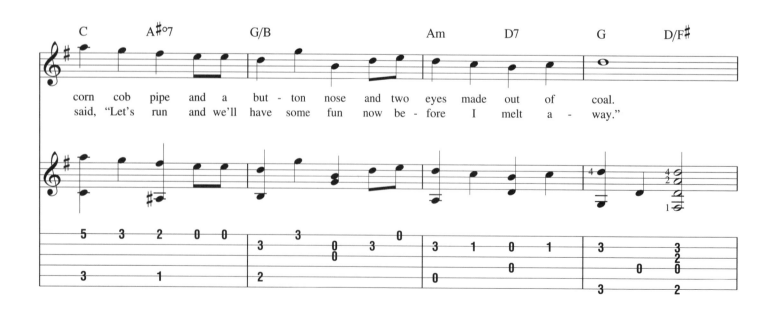

Verse

Fros - ty the snow man was a - live as he could be, and the
Fros - ty the snow man had to hur - ry on his way, but he

chil - dren say he could laugh and play just the same as you and me.
waved good - bye say - in', "Don't you cry, I'll be back a - gain some day."

Outro

Thump - et - y thump thump, thump - et - y thump thump, look at Fros - ty go.

Thump - et - y thump thump, thump - et - y thump thump, o - ver the hills of snow.

14

Happy Xmas

(War Is Over)

Words and Music by John Lennon and Yoko Ono

Drop D tuning:
(low to high) D-A-D-G-B-E

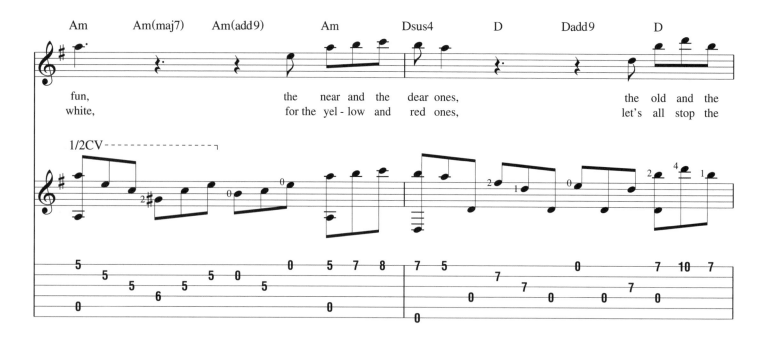

fun,
white,

the near and the dear ones,
for the yel - low and red ones,

the old and the
let's all stop the

Chorus

young. ____
fights. ____

A mer - ry, mer-ry Christ - mas ____

and a hap - py new

year,

let's hope it's a good one _____

with - out an - y

fear.   2., 3. And so this is   fear.

Outro

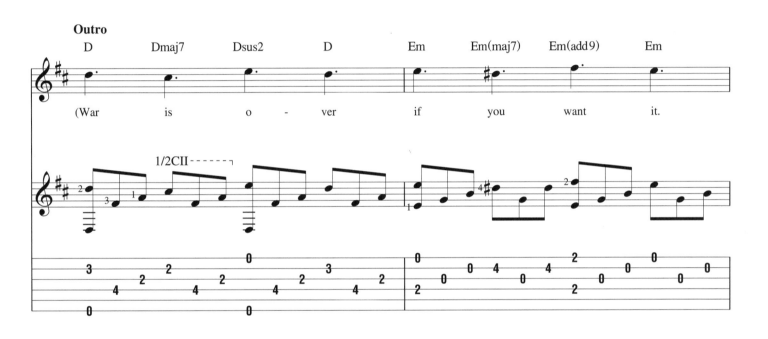

(War   is   o - ver   if   you   want   it.

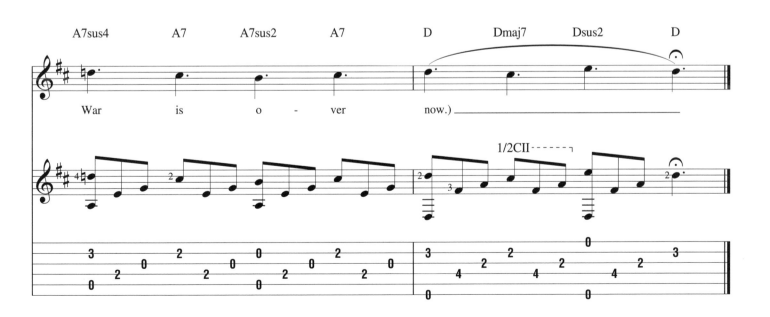

War   is   o - ver   now.)

Happy Holiday

from the Motion Picture Irving Berlin's HOLIDAY INN

Words and Music by Irving Berlin

1. Hap - py hol - i - day, _____ hap - py hol - i - day. _____

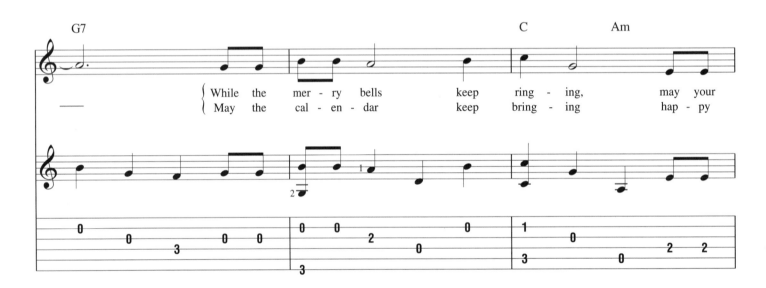

While the mer - ry bells keep ring - ing, may your
May the cal - en - dar keep bring - ing hap - py

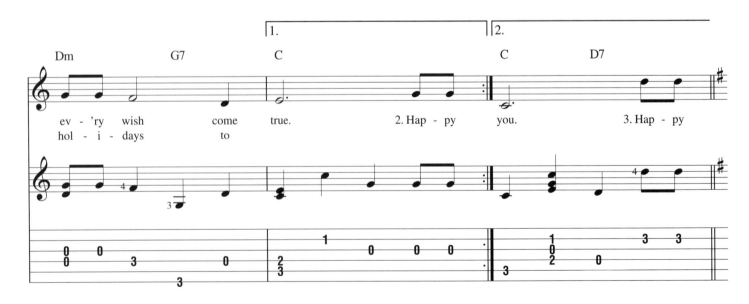

ev - 'ry wish come true.   2. Hap - py   you.   3. Hap - py
hol - i - days   to

Verse

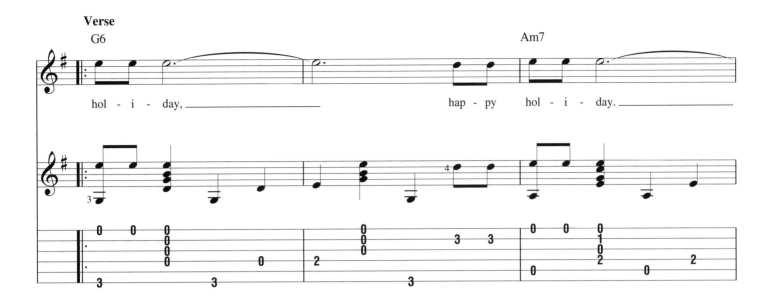

hol - i - day, _____ hap - py hol - i - day. _____

While the mer - ry bells keep ring - ing, may your
May the cal - en - dar keep bring - ing hap - py

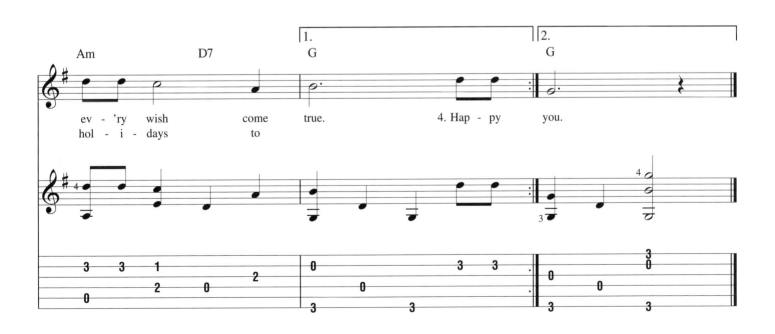

ev - 'ry wish come true. 4. Hap - py you.
hol - i - days come to

Here Comes Santa Claus
(Right Down Santa Claus Lane)

Words and Music by Gene Autry and Oakley Haldeman

Additional Lyrics

3. Here comes Santa Claus, here comes Santa Claus,
   Right down Santa Claus Lane.
   He doesn't care if you're rich or poor,
   For he loves you just the same.
   Santa knows that we're God's children,
   That makes ev'rything right.
   Fill your hearts with Christmas cheer,
   'Cause Santa Claus comes tonight.

4. Here comes Santa Claus, here comes Santa Claus,
   Right down Santa Claus Lane.
   He'll come around when the chimes ring out,
   It's Christmas morn again.
   Peace on earth will come to all
   If we just follow the light.
   Let's give thanks to the Lord above.
   'Cause Santa Claus comes tonight,
   'Cause Santa Claus comes tonight.

A Holly Jolly Christmas

Music and Lyrics by Johnny Marks

1. Have a (4.) hol - ly jol - ly Christ - mas, it's the best time of the year.

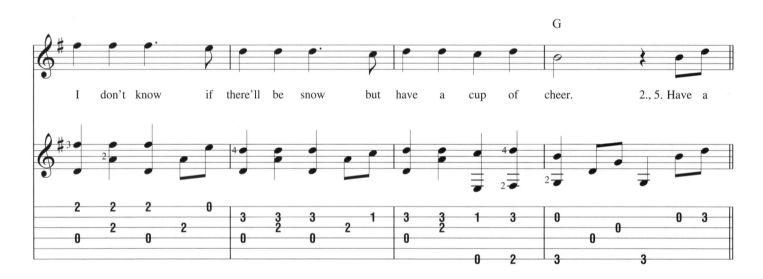

I don't know if there'll be snow but have a cup of cheer. 2., 5. Have a

hol - ly jol - ly Christ - mas, and when you walk down the street,

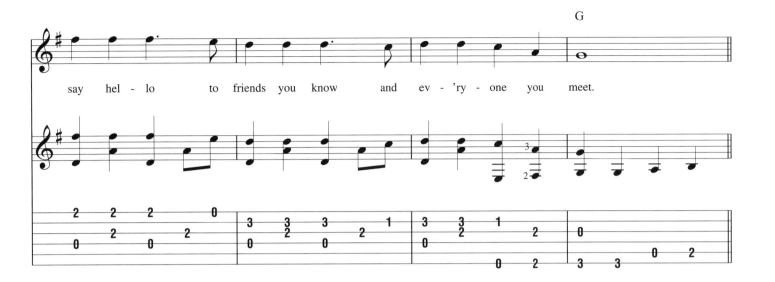

say hel - lo   to friends you know   and ev - 'ry - one you meet.

Bridge

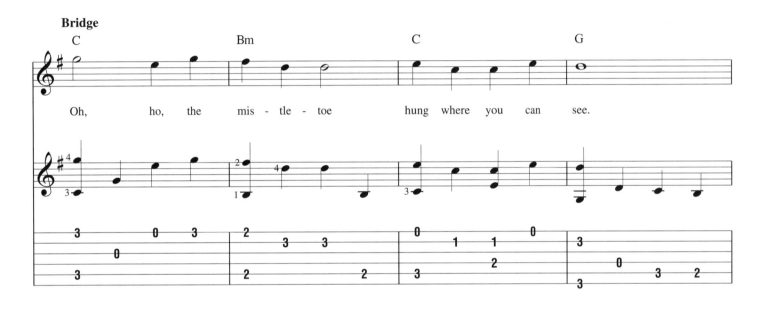

Oh,   ho,   the mis - tle - toe   hung where you can   see.

Some - bod - y waits for you,   kiss her once for me.   3., 6. Have a

Verse

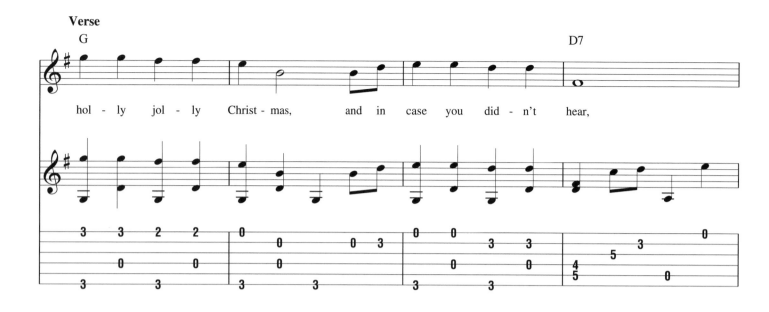

hol - ly jol - ly Christ - mas, and in case you did - n't hear,

oh, by gol - ly, have a hol - ly jol - ly Christ - mas this year. 4. Have a

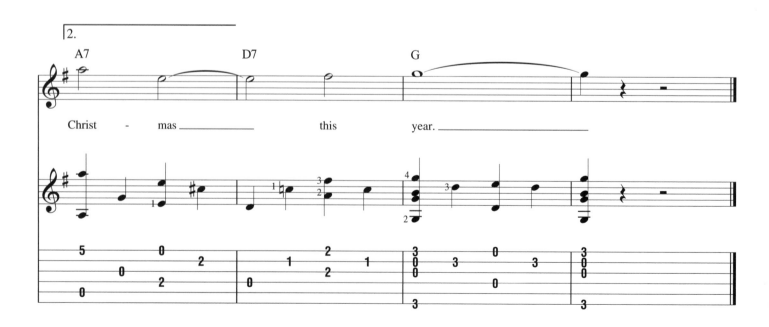

Christ - mas _____ this year. _____

Jingle-Bell Rock

Words and Music by Joe Beal and Jim Boothe

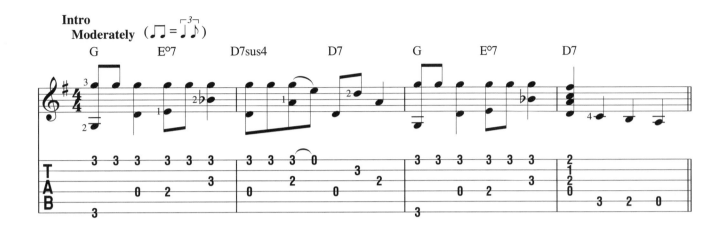

I Saw Mommy Kissing Santa Claus

Words and Music by Tommie Connor

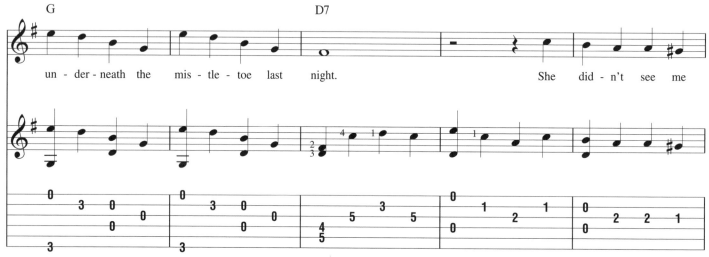

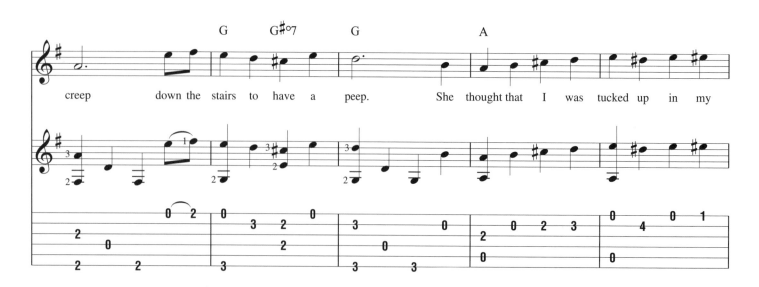

I'll Be Home for Christmas

Words and Music by Kim Gannon and Walter Kent

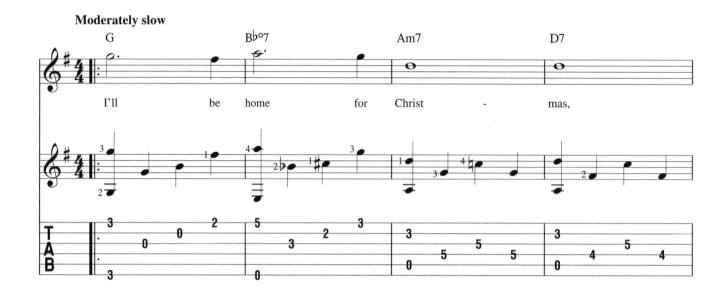

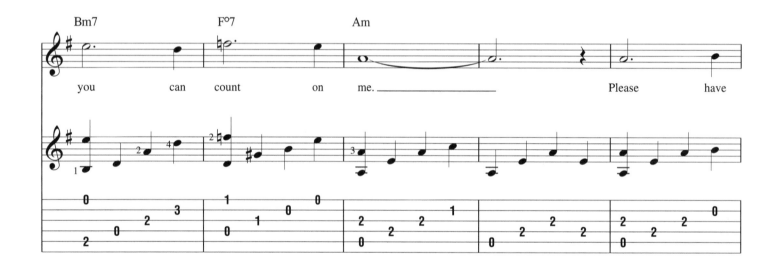

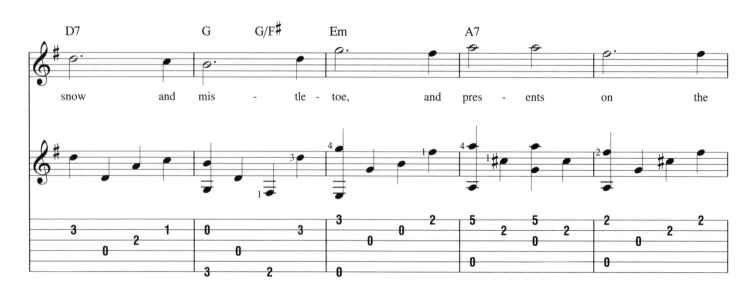

Let It Snow! Let It Snow! Let It Snow!

Words by Sammy Cahn
Music by Jule Styne

Bridge

fin - al - ly kiss good - night, how I'll hate go - ing out in the

storm. But if you'll real - ly hold me tight,

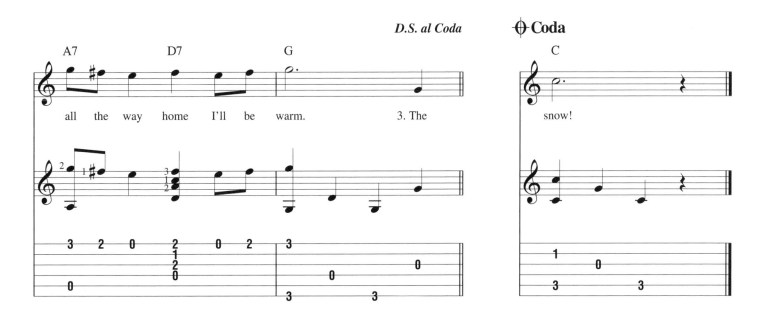

D.S. al Coda   **Coda**

all the way home I'll be warm.   3. The   snow!

Merry Christmas, Darling

Words and Music by Richard Carpenter and Frank Pooler

Silver Bells

from the Paramount Picture THE LEMON DROP KID

Words and Music by Jay Livingston and Ray Evans

Verse

Moderately

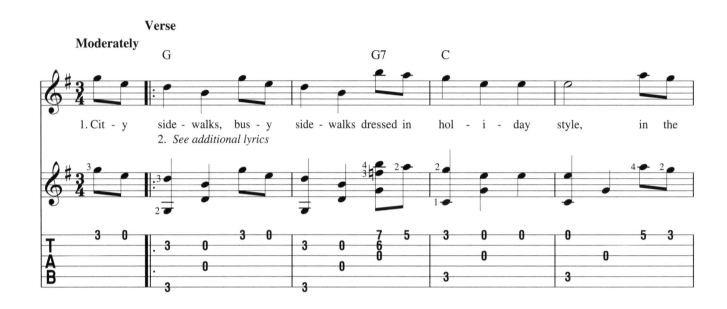

1. Cit - y side - walks, bus - y side - walks dressed in hol - i - day style, in the
2. *See additional lyrics*

air there's a feel - ing ___ of Christ - mas. ___ Chil - dren laugh - ing, peo - ple pass - ing, meet - ing

smile af - ter smile, and on ev - 'ry street cor - ner you hear: ___

Chorus

Additional Lyrics

2. Strings of street lights, even stop lights
   Blink a bright red and green,
   As the shoppers rush home with their treasures.
   Hear the snow crunch, see the kids bunch,
   This is Santa's big scene.
   And above all the bustle you hear:

This Christmas

Words and Music by Donny Hathaway and Nadine McKinnor

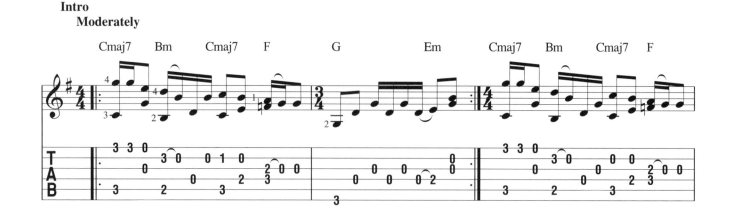

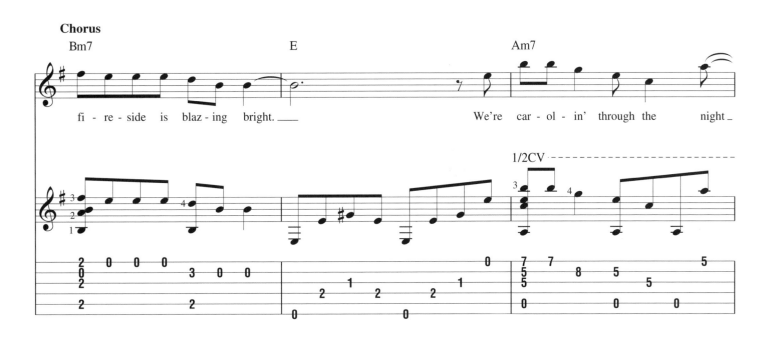

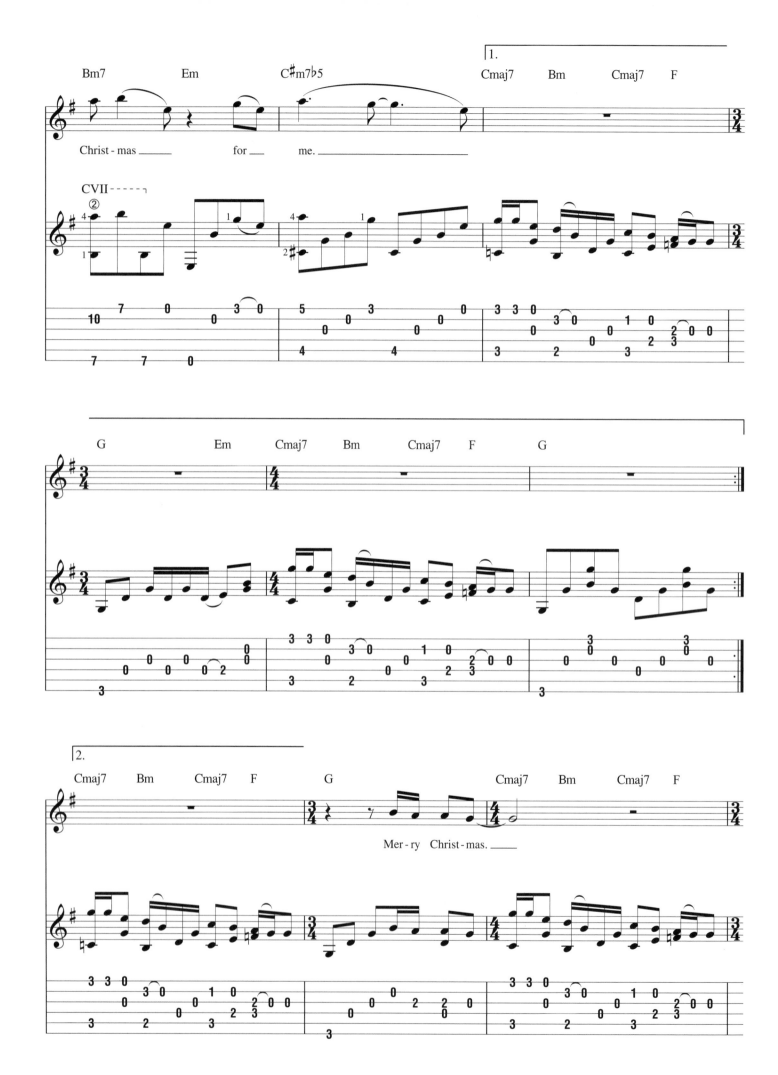

Rudolph the Red-Nosed Reindeer

Music and Lyrics by Johnny Marks

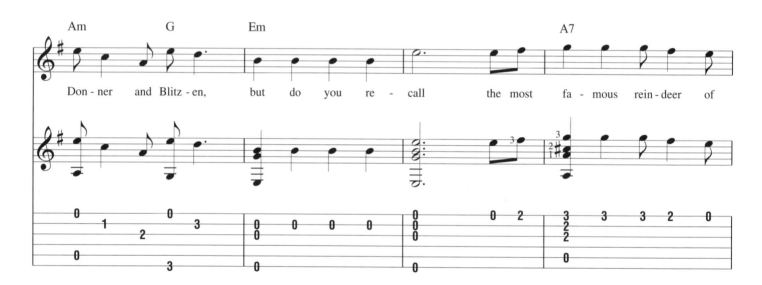

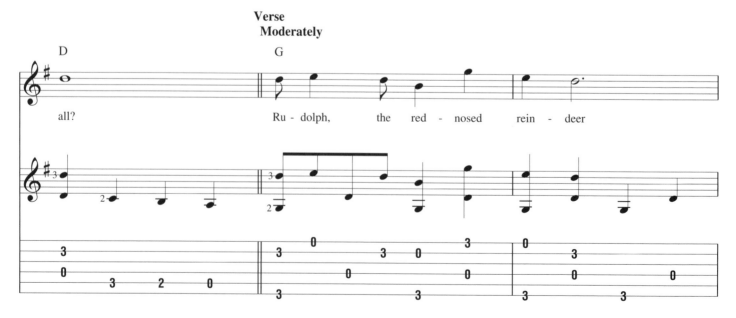

Outro

GUITAR SONGBOOKS FOR THE HOLIDAYS

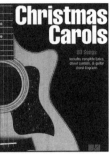  

THE BIG CHRISTMAS COLLECTION FOR EASY GUITAR

Includes over 70 Christmas favorites, such as: Ave Maria • Blue Christmas • Deck the Hall • Feliz Navidad • Frosty the Snow Man • Happy Holiday • A Holly Jolly Christmas • Joy to the World • O Holy Night • Silver and Gold • Suzy Snowflake • You're All I Want for Christmas • and more.
00698978 Easy Guitar with Notes and Tab $16.95 **INCLUDES TAB**

CHRISTMAS CHEER FOR EASY GUITAR

26 songs, including: Blue Christmas • The Christmas Song (Chestnuts Roasting) • Frosty, the Snow Man • Happy Xmas • It's Beginning to Look Like Christmas • Rudolph the Red-Nosed Reindeer • Wonderful Christmastime • and more.
00702048 Easy Guitar with Notes and Tab $10.95 **INCLUDES TAB**

CHRISTMAS CLASSICS

Over 25 easy guitar arrangements of Christmas favorites: Auld Lang Syne • Away in a Manger • Deck the Hall • The First Noel • I Saw Three Ships • Jingle Bells • O Christmas Tree • Once in a Royal David's City • Silent Night • Up on the Housetop • What Child Is This? • and more. Easy guitar arrangements in standard notation and tablature.
00702028 Easy Guitar with Notes and Tab $7.95 **INCLUDES TAB**

CHRISTMAS FAVORITES - 2ND EDITION

A collection of 33 seasonal songs in standard notation and tab. Includes: Angels We Have Heard on High • The First Noel • I Saw Three Ships • Joy to the World • O Come All Ye Faithful • O Holy Night • What Child Is This • and more.
00699097 Easy Guitar with Notes and Tab $9.95 **INCLUDES TAB**

CHRISTMAS TIDINGS

23 easy arrangements of Christmas favorites, including: Blue Christmas • The Chipmunk Song • Feliz Navidad • Grandma Got Run Over by a Reindeer • Happy Holiday • I'll Be Home for Christmas • Rudolph the Red-Nosed Reindeer • Silver Bells • and more.
00699123 Easy Guitar with Notes and Tab $9.95 **INCLUDES TAB**

CONTEMPORARY CHRISTIAN CHRISTMAS

19 contemporary favorites recorded by top artists: Breath of Heaven (Mary's song) • Celebrate the Child • Child of Bethlehem • Emmanuel • Good News • Jesus is Born • One Small Child • Precious Promise • A Strange Way to Save the World • This Gift • This Little Child • and more.
00702170 Easy Guitar with Notes and Tab $9.95 **INCLUDES TAB**

CHRISTMAS CAROLS — GUITAR CHORD SONGBOOK

Includes complete lyrics, chord symbols, and guitar chord diagrams. A convenient reference of 80 Christmas carols for the player who just needs the lyrics and chords. Songs include: Angels We Have Heard on High • Away in a Manger • Deck the Hall • Good King Wenceslas • The Holly and the Ivy • I Heard the Bells on Christmas Day • Jingle Bells • Joy to the World • O Holy Night • Silent Night • Up on the Housetop • We Wish You a Merry Christmas • Welsh Carol • What Child Is This? • and more.
00699536 Guitar Chords/Lyrics $12.95

CHRISTMAS SONGS FOR GUITAR

The Strum It! series lets guitar players strum the chords (and sing along) with their favorite songs. The songs in each book have been selected because they can be played with regular open chords, barre chords, or other moveable chord types. All songs are shown in their original keys complete with chords, strum patterns, melody and lyrics. This book features over 45 Christmas favorites, including: The Christmas Song (Chestnuts Roasting on an Open Fire) • Feliz Navidad • Frosty the Snow Man • Grandma Got Run over by a Reindeer • The Greatest Gift of All • (There's No Place Like) Home for the Holidays • I'll Be Home for Christmas • It's Beginning to Look like Christmas • The Most Wonderful Time of the Year • Rockin' Around the Christmas Tree • Rudolph the Red-Nosed Reindeer • Silver Bells • and more.
00699247 Strum It Guitar $9.95

A FINGERSTYLE GUITAR CHRISTMAS

Over 20 songs for fingerstyle guitar: Auld Lang Syne • Ave Maria • Away in a Manger • The Coventry Carol • Dec.k the Hall • The First Noel • Good King Wenceslas • I Saw Three Ships • Joy to the World • Silent Night • Up on the Housetop • What Child Is This? • and more.
00699038 Fingerstyle Guitar $12.95 **INCLUDES TAB**

THE GUITAR STRUMMER'S CHRISTMAS SONGBOOK

A great collection of 80 favorite Christmas tunes that can be played with open chords, barre chords or other moveable chord types - all in their original keys, complete with chords, strum patterns, melody and lyrics. Includes: The Christmas Song (Chestnuts Roasting on an Open Fire) • Christmas Time Is Here • Do They Know It's Christmas? • Feliz Navidad • Frosty the Snow Man • Grandma Got Run over by a Reindeer • A Holly Jolly Christmas • I Heard the Bells on Christmas Day • I've Got My Love to Keep Me Warm • It's Christmas in New York • Let It Snow! Let It Snow! Let It Snow! • My Favorite Things • O Holy Night • Rudolph the Red-Nosed Reindeer • Silver Bells • We Wish You a Merry Christmas • You Make It Feel like Christmas • and more.
00699527 Melody/Lyrics/Chords $14.95

HAPPY HOLIDAY

20 holiday favorites arranged for fingerstyle guitar, including: Happy Holiday • I'll Be Home for Christmas • My Favorite Things • Rockin' Around the Christmas Tree • Silver Bells • and more.
00699209 Fingerstyle Guitar $10.95 **INCLUDES TAB**

LET IT SNOW!

22 songs for fingerstyle guitar, including: Blue Christmas • The Christmas Song (Chestnuts Roasting on an Open Fire) • Feliz Navidad • Frosty the Snow Man • Jingle-Bell Rock • We Need a Little Christmas • and more.
00699206 Fingerstyle Guitar $10.95 **INCLUDES TAB**

Prices, contents, and availability subject to change without notice.

FOR MORE INFORMATION, SEE YOUR LOCAL MUSIC DEALER,
OR WRITE TO:

HAL•LEONARD®
CORPORATION
7777 W. BLUEMOUND RD. P.O. BOX 13819 MILWAUKEE, WI 53213

www.halleonard.com

0703

GUITAR PLAY-ALONG

This series will help you play your favorite songs quickly and easily. Just follow the tab and listen to the CD to hear how the guitar should sound, and then play along using the separate backing tracks. Mac or PC users can also slow down the tempo by using the CD in their computer. The melody and lyrics are also included in the book so that you can sing or simply follow along.

INCLUDES TAB

VOL. 1 – ROCK GUITAR   00699570 / $12.95
Day Tripper • Message in a Bottle • Refugee • Shattered • Sunshine of Your Love • Takin' Care of Business • Tush • Walk This Way.

VOL. 2 – ACOUSTIC   00699569 / $12.95
Angie • Behind Blue Eyes • Best of My Love • Blackbird • Dust in the Wind • Layla • Night Moves • Yesterday.

VOL. 3 – HARD ROCK   00699573 / $14.95
Crazy Train • Iron Man • Living After Midnight • Rock You Like a Hurricane • Round and Round • Smoke on the Water • Sweet Child O' Mine • You Really Got Me.

VOL. 4 – POP/ROCK   00699571 / $12.95
Breakdown • Crazy Little Thing Called Love • Hit Me with Your Best Shot • I Want You to Want Me • Lights • R.O.C.K. in the U.S.A. (A Salute to 60's Rock) • Summer of '69 • What I Like About You.

VOL. 5 – MODERN ROCK   00699574 / $12.95
Aerials • Alive • Bother • Chop Suey! • Control • Last Resort • Take a Look Around (Theme from "M:I-2") • Wish You Were Here.

VOL. 6 – '90S ROCK   00699572 / $12.95
Are You Gonna Go My Way • Come Out and Play • I'll Stick Around • Know Your Enemy • Man in the Box • Outshined • Smells Like Teen Spirit • Under the Bridge.

VOL. 7 – BLUES GUITAR   00699575 / $12.95
All Your Love (I Miss Loving) • Born Under a Bad Sign • Hide Away • I'm Tore Down • I'm Your Hoochie Coochie Man • Pride and Joy • Sweet Home Chicago • The Thrill Is Gone.

VOL. 8 – ROCK   00699585 / $12.95
All Right Now • Black Magic Woman • Get Back • Hey Joe • Layla • Love Me Two Times • Won't Get Fooled Again • You Really Got Me.

VOL. 9 – PUNK ROCK   00699576 / $12.95
All the Small Things • Fat Lip • Flavor of the Weak • I Feel So • Lifestyles of the Rich and Famous • (So) Tired of Waiting for You • Say It Ain't So • Self Esteem.

VOL. 10 – ACOUSTIC   00699586 / $12.95
Here Comes the Sun • Landslide • The Magic Bus • Norwegian Wood (This Bird Has Flown) • Pink Houses • Space Oddity • Tangled Up in Blue • Tears in Heaven.

VOL. 11 – EARLY ROCK   00699579 / $12.95
Fun, Fun, Fun • Hound Dog • Louie, Louie • No Particular Place to Go • Oh, Pretty Woman • Rock Around the Clock • Under the Boardwalk • Wild Thing.

VOL. 12 – POP/ROCK   00699587 / $12.95
867-5309/Jenny • Every Breath You Take • Money for Nothing • Rebel, Rebel • Run to You • Ticket to Ride • Wonderful Tonight • You Give Love a Bad Name.

VOL. 13 – FOLK ROCK   00699581 / $12.95
Annie's Song • Leaving on a Jet Plane • Suite: Judy Blue Eyes • This Land Is Your Land • Time in a Bottle • Turn! Turn! Turn! (To Everything There Is a Season) • You've Got a Friend • You've Got to Hide Your Love Away.

VOL. 14 – BLUES ROCK   00699582 / $14.95
Blue on Black • Crossfire • Cross Road Blues (Crossroads) • The House Is Rockin' • La Grange • Move It on Over • Roadhouse Blues • Statesboro Blues.

VOL. 15 – R&B   00699583 / $12.95
Ain't Too Proud to Beg • Brick House • Get Ready • I Can't Help Myself (Sugar Pie, Honey Bunch) • I Got You (I Feel Good) • I Heard It Through the Grapevine • My Girl • Shining Star.

VOL. 16 – JAZZ   00699584 / $12.95
All Blues • Bluesette • Footprints • How Insensitive (Insensatez) • Misty • Satin Doll • Stella by Starlight • Tenor Madness.

VOL. 17 – COUNTRY   00699588 / $12.95
Amie • Boot Scootin' Boogie • Chattahoochee • Folsom Prison Blues • Friends in Low Places • Forever and Ever, Amen • T-R-O-U-B-L-E • Workin' Man Blues.

VOL. 18 – ACOUSTIC ROCK   00699577 / $14.95
About a Girl • Breaking the Girl • Drive • Iris • More Than Words • Patience • Silent Lucidity • 3 AM.

VOL. 19 – SOUL   00699578 / $12.95
Get Up (I Feel Like Being) a Sex Machine • Green Onions • In the Midnight Hour • Knock on Wood • Mustang Sally • Respect • (Sittin' On) the Dock of the Bay • Soul Man.

VOL. 20 – ROCKABILLY   00699580 / $12.95
Be-Bop-A-Lula • Blue Suede Shoes • Hello Mary Lou • Little Sister • Mystery Train • Rock This Town • Stray Cat Strut • That'll Be the Day.

VOL. 21 – YULETIDE   00699602 / $12.95
Angels We Have Heard on High • Away in a Manger • Deck the Hall • The First Noel • Go, Tell It on the Mountain • Jingle Bells • Joy to the World • O Little Town of Bethlehem.

VOL. 22 – CHRISTMAS   00699600 / $12.95
The Christmas Song (Chestnuts Roasting on an Open Fire) • Frosty the Snow Man • Happy Xmas (War Is Over) • Here Comes Santa Claus (Right Down Santa Claus Lane) • Jingle-Bell Rock • Merry Christmas, Darling • Rudolph the Red-Nosed Reindeer • Silver Bells.

VOL. 23 – SURF   00699635 / $12.95
Let's Go Trippin' • Out of Limits • Penetration • Pipeline • Surf City • Surfin' U.S.A. • Walk Don't Run • The Wedge.

VOL. 24 – ERIC CLAPTON   00699649 / $14.95
Badge • Bell Bottom Blues • Change the World • Cocaine • Key to the Highway • Lay Down Sally • White Room • Wonderful Tonight.

VOL. 25 – LENNON AND McCARTNEY   00699642 / $14.95
Back in the U.S.S.R. • Drive My Car • Get Back • A Hard Day's Night • I Feel Fine • Paperback Writer • Revolution • Ticket to Ride.

VOL. 26 – ELVIS PRESLEY   00699643 / $14.95
All Shook Up • Blue Suede Shoes • Don't Be Cruel (To a Heart That's True) • Heartbreak Hotel • Hound Dog • Jailhouse Rock • Little Sister • Mystery Train.

VOL. 27 – DAVID LEE ROTH   00699645 / $14.95
Ain't Talkin' 'Bout Love • Dance the Night Away • Just Like Paradise • A Lil' Ain't Enough • Panama • Runnin' with the Devil • Unchained • Yankee Rose.

VOL. 28 – GREG KOCH   00699646 / $14.95
Chief's Blues • Death of a Bassman • Dylan the Villain • The Grip • Holy Grail • Spank It • Tonus Diabolicus • Zoiks.

VOL. 29 – BOB SEGER   00699647 / $14.95
Against the Wind • Betty Lou's Gettin' Out Tonight • Hollywood Nights • Mainstreet • Night Moves • Old Time Rock & Roll • Rock and Roll Never Forgets • Still the Same.

VOL. 30 – KISS   00699644 / $14.95
Cold Gin • Detroit Rock City • Deuce • Firehouse • Heaven's on Fire • Love Gun • Rock and Roll All Nite • Shock Me.

VOL. 31 – CHRISTMAS HITS   00699652 / $12.95
Blue Christmas • Do You Hear What I Hear • Happy Holiday • I Saw Mommy Kissing Santa Claus • I'll Be Home for Christmas • Let It Snow! Let It Snow! Let It Snow! • Little Saint Nick • Snowfall.

Prices, contents, and availability subject to change without notice.

FOR MORE INFORMATION, SEE YOUR LOCAL MUSIC DEALER,
OR WRITE TO:

**HAL•LEONARD®
CORPORATION**
7777 W. BLUEMOUND RD. P.O. BOX 13819 MILWAUKEE, WI 53213

Visit Hal Leonard online at www.halleonard.com

0604

Playdays

annual 1996

Hello!

The Playdays Annual is now five years old and it
just keeps getting better and better every year!
Your Playdays friends are waiting inside,
so don't delay, turn the pages
for hours of fun and happy reading.

This annual is based on the BBC television programme
Playdays produced by Felgate Productions Ltd
for BBC television.
The BBC logotype and the Playdays logotype are Trademarks
of the British Broadcasting Corporation.
"BBC" and "Playdays" are Registered Trademarks of the British
Broadcasting Corporation.
All Trademarks are used under non-exclusive licence.

Text © Felgate Productions Ltd., 1995
Written and compiled by Christina Takkides and
Clare Bradley

Edited by Margaret McCarthy
Designed by Liz Auger

Illustrated by Jeannette Slater, Kristina Stephenson, Paul
Johnson, Ken Morton, Sonia Canals and Robin Lawrie

Cover photograph by Christopher Baines
Photographs by Sally Miles and Adam Freidman

Published in Great Britain by World International,
an imprint of Egmont Publishing Ltd., Egmont House, PO Box 111
Great Ducie Street, Manchester M60 3BL.
Printed in Italy.
ISBN 0 7498 2397 6

Contents

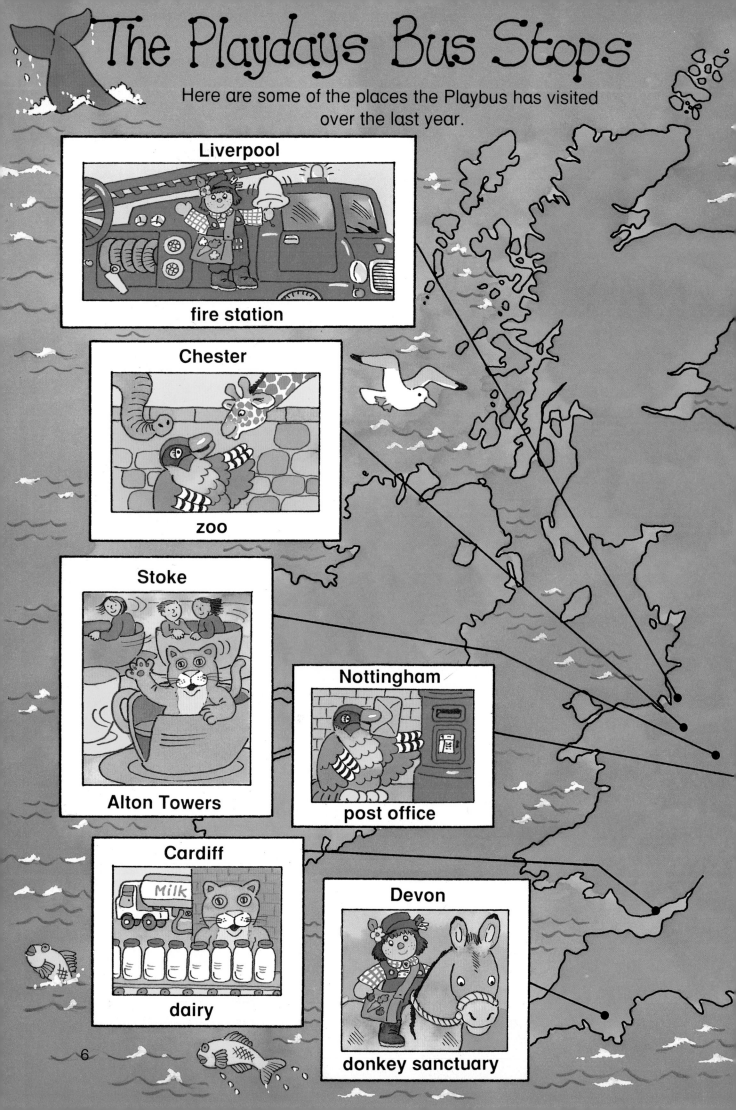

The Playdays Bus Stops

Here are some of the places the Playbus has visited over the last year.

Liverpool

fire station

Chester

zoo

Stoke

Alton Towers

Nottingham

post office

Cardiff

dairy

Devon

donkey sanctuary

6

York

doll's house

Hull

airport

Northampton

canal

Bedfordshire

safari park

New Forest

Isle of Wight

seaside

Has the Playbus stopped near where you live?

Look out! It could be visiting your town, soon!

Peggy and Poppy and Why

Three friends are we
We're on TV,
Peggy and Poppy and Why.
Everyone knows us
We go on the Playbus,
Peggy and Poppy and Why.

Why is the Why Bird,
She's green and she's red.
Peggy wears pegs
In the hat on her head.
Poppy loves sardines
Or, so it is said,
Peggy and Poppy and Why.

Can you colour us in?

8

Why Bird's favourite things

Food: Anything and everything - well, almost!

Colour: Red and green - like my feathers.

Number: 3 because Peggy, Poppy and me add up to 3.

Animal: Poppy the cat.

Song: 'The Owl and the Pussycat.'

Story: 'The Little Red Hen.'

Book: 'The Playdays Annual.'

TV programme: Playdays - the Why Bird stop

Out and About

Can you find all the items in the picture?
As you find them, tick the boxes.

bus
stop

11

A picture for Aunt Helen by Valerie Bond

Josie sat at the painting table wondering what to paint.

Dean, sitting next to her, was painting a hot, steamy jungle .

Opposite, Tim was painting a little red boat being tossed about on a dark blue sea.

Mrs Foster came to see how they were getting on.

"Oh, Josie," she said. "You haven't painted anything yet, and it's nearly time to pack up and go home!"

"I can't think what to paint," said Josie. "And I promised Aunt Helen I'd paint a picture for her today to put on her kitchen wall."

"What sort of picture would Aunt Helen like?" asked Mrs Foster.

"A jungle like mine," suggested Dean, holding up his picture. It was green and brown and full of tall, leafy trees and long wiggly snakes.

Josie shook her head. Aunt Helen didn't like snakes.

12

"Paint her a boat like mine," suggested Tim.

Josie shook her head. Boats made Aunt Helen seasick.

"Try painting the first thing that comes into your mind, Josie," suggested Mrs Foster.

Josie painted a big, thick, bright yellow blob.

"What's that?" asked Tim.

"I don't know," replied Josie. "It was the first thing that came into my mind."

"Make it into something, Josie," said Mrs Foster, moving away. "But do it quickly."

"What sort of something?" asked Josie.

13

"Make it into the sun," suggested Sarah, coming to see if she could help.

"Make it into a leopard," suggested Ali, as he appeared from under the table. "Paint some legs and a head. Put black spots all over it. Then it will be a great roaring leopard, just like me!" Ali roared off on all fours around the room.

"Make it into a football," suggested Rachel. "Paint some grass here, and a girl there, kicking it. Then it will be just like me scoring goals against my Dad in the park." Rachel kicked her leg high in the air.

Josie sighed. So many ideas, but they weren't her ideas. She wanted to paint a special picture for Aunt Helen, and she wanted to do it on her own.

School

Josie sat and stared at the bright yellow blob on the paper. It was big and round, with some thick, lumpy bits of paint in it.

"What could it be?" thought Josie. And then Josie had an idea; her very own idea!

A few minutes later, when it was time to go home, Aunt Helen came to collect Josie.

"May I see your picture, Josie?" Mrs Foster asked as Josie was about to leave.

Josie proudly showed her picture to Mrs Foster. There, on the paper was the big, thick, bright yellow blob. But that was all. There was nothing else.

"Why didn't you make it into something?" asked Mrs Foster, puzzled.

"I didn't need to," replied Josie. "It was something already."

"Oh!" said Mrs Foster, even more puzzled. "What sort of something?"

"Bananas and custard!" said Josie.

"My favourite!" said Aunt Helen, who was quite delighted. "What a perfect picture. Let's go home and put it on my kitchen wall straight away."

"And then what will we do?" asked Josie.

"Then we'll make some real bananas and custard," laughed Aunt Helen. "Your wonderful picture has made me feel quite hungry, Josie!"

Find the Pairs

A pair is when 2 things are the same as each other.
Can you see 6 pairs?

The Playdays Year

In **January** wrap up tight.
Go in the snow for a snowball fight.

February's a mystery –
A Valentine card arrives for me.

March brings wind and rain all day.
Whoops! My hat has blown away!

In **April** I wear my Easter bonnet
With chicks and flowers and rabbits on it.

In **May** the world is turning green
And I become the May Queen.

In **June** I dress in my running shorts,
I'm taking part in the school sports.

July is for holidays, pack up the cases
We're travelling off to far away places.

In **August** you'll find me out on the sand
With a lovely, cold ice-cream in my hand.

When **September** comes it's off to school
And Autumn leaves turn red and fall.

October is misty - oh, where can I be?
The fog is so thick, I can hardly see!

In **November** we have bonfire night.
Whoops-a-daisy! What a fright!

December means that Christmas is near
And when it is over we start a new year!

Milkround

The  stops outside .

She has left a asking for

and .

The next stop is at .

Her asks for and

.

wants to make

on for her .

20

The  stops at  .

She has ordered  to drink

and  for her  .

As the  leaves,

comes to the  and asks for

some  .

What would you order from your

?

21

Make a bubbly Jellyfish!
with Morris and Milly

What do we need, Milly?
To make two jellyfish - we'll need:
a plastic tub
a piece of card
washing up liquid
paint
some strips of paper
glue
a straw

1. Put a 1/4 cup of washing up liquid and some paint into the tub.

2. Use the straw to blow - carefully, Morris!

3. Blow until the bubbles overflow the tub.

4. Gently put the card onto the bubbles.

5. You can do it more than once, or use other colours, too.

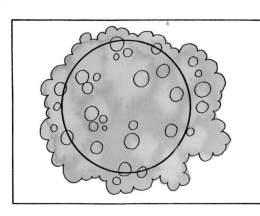

6. Leave the bubble print to dry. Then, ask a grown-up to cut a circle from it.

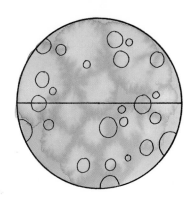

7. Cut the circle in half.

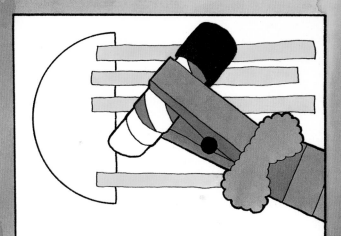

8. On the back of each half stick some paper strips.

9. Now draw or paint some eyes.

23

Larrington Lion   by Trish Cooke

In a jungle, far away, lived a very beautiful lion called Larrington.
Everyone thought he was beautiful - including Larrington himself!
In fact, Larrington was so proud of his good looks that he often sang
about them:

> "Oh! what a charming creature I must be
> My beauty is so rare.
> I'm such a proud and pretty lion
> With my coat of wavy hair."

One morning, Larrington came across Tina Tiger. "Good morning,
Larrington," said Tina, politely. "Your coat looks very fine today. Very
fine indeed."
"Yes, my coat is lovely," agreed Larrington, graciously.
Tina sighed. "I wish my hair was long and wavy like that, instead it's
short and stripy."
Larrington smiled to himself as he walked on, feeling even more
proud. Then he began to sing again:

> "Oh! what a charming creature I must be
> My beauty is so rare.
> I'm such a proud and pretty lion
> With my coat of wavy hair."

A little further on, Larrington met Terry Turtle.

"Good morning, Larrington," said Terry. "Your coat looks very nice today."

"Yes, it does," replied Larrington, happy that once again his marvellous coat had been noticed.

The turtle sighed. "I wish I had hair like yours but I have no hair, so I hide my head in my back."

"I can see that," said Larrington. And once again he roared with laughter and sang his favourite song:

"Oh! what a charming creature I must be
My beauty is so rare.
I'm such a proud and pretty lion
With my coat of wavy hair."

25

By now it was the afternoon - the hottest part of the day in the jungle. All the animals settled down to take a nice cool rest. Larrington settled down, too, but it was very hot and try as he might, he just couldn't get comfortable.

The sun shone even brighter. Terry Turtle and Tina Tiger snoozed happily, but Larrington was feeling very hot and bothered.

He tried blowing his hair away from his face, but it just bounced back into the thick strong mane he was usually so proud of.

"I'm hot," roared Larrington. "Very, very hot."

Just then, Ella Elephant strolled by.

"Good afternoon, Larrington," said Ella, politely.

"Oh, hello," grunted Larrington.

Ella walked on.

"Excuse me," called Larrington.

"Yes," said Ella, turning back.

"Don't you have something to say to me?"

Ella thought for a moment.

"No," she said, finally. "I don't think so."

Larrington was almost speechless...but not quite. "But don't you like my coat of wavy hair?"

"Oh, I suppose," said Ella.

"You suppose?" repeated Larrington.

"Yes, I suppose it's OK for a lion."

By now, Larrington was very hot and bothered, and even more annoyed. Larrington persisted. "But don't you wish you had hair like mine?"

Ella Elephant stood back and looked at this hot and angry lion before her.

"And why would I want hair like yours, Larrington?" said Ella, amazed. "I'm an elephant, not a lion. My Great Uncle Mammoth had hair a long time ago but it got in the way. I much prefer to be bald. It's so much cooler."

"Cooler?" asked Larrington.

"Oh, yes," called Tina Tiger. "It's much cooler without long hair."

"Yes, I quite agree," said Terry Turtle. "I'm very cool in my shell."

For the first time, Larrington wished he did not have such long and wavy hair. It made him so very hot.

27

Ella smiled at this rather proud lion as he panted in the burning sun.

"Would you like me to give you a shower?" she asked, looking at the pond behind them.

Larrington nodded. "Yes, please, Ella," he said. "That would be very nice."

Ella dipped her trunk in the pond and sucked in as much water as she could. Then she turned slowly, raised her trunk and blew the water all over Larrington.

Larrington sighed with relief and then shook and jumped around. "Oooh! It's lovely," he said. And then he began to sing again:

"What charming creatures we must be
Our beauty is so rare.
I'm such a pretty lion,
Tina's such a pretty tiger,
Terry's such a pretty turtle,
Ella's such a pretty elephant
With or without hair."

Everyone laughed and joined in the singing.

Feeding Time

Can you help each animal find their food?

29

Playing Shops

How many buns has Mr Jolly got in his baker's shop?

5 currant buns at the Roundabout Stop
Sticky and fat with a cherry on top.
Along came Why with a penny one day...

...bought a currant bun and took it away.

How many buns has Mr Jolly got left now?

Yes **4**!

 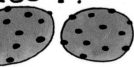

4 currant buns at the Roundabout Stop
Sticky and fat with a cherry on top.
Along came Peggy with a penny
one day bought a currant bun and
took it away.

How many buns are left now?

Yes **3**!

3 currant buns at the Roundabout Stop
Sticky and fat with a cherry on top.
Along came Poppy with a penny one day
bought a currant bun and took it away.

How many buns are left now?

Yes **2**!

2 currant buns at the Roundabout Stop
Sticky and fat with a cherry on top.
Along came Lizzie with a penny one day
bought a currant bun and took it away.

How many buns has
Mr Jolly got left?

Yes **1**!

And this one's for me!

Why's shopping list

Can you help me find all the things on my list?

cakes

biscuits

apples

pears

sardines

bananas

carrots

milk

bread

cheese

crisps

only 10P

50P off!

Cakes

Dairy

Sardines! Sardines! Sardines!

Crisps Crisps Crisps Crisps

Milk Milk Mil

Cola Cola Cola Col

Milk

33

Peggy's bug Patch

When you are outside see how
many insects you can find.
Here are some to look out for.

dragonfly

fly

wasp

bee

earwig

butterfly

grasshopper

caterpillar

ladybird

Do you know which two creatures are the same?

Answer: The caterpillar changes into a butterfly.

34

Peggy's favourite things

Food: All vegetables, especially potatoes!

Colour: Blue - like my trousers and hat and the sky.

Number: 8 because it is the same shape when it stands on its head.

Animal: I love all animals but if I had to choose one it would be a rabbit as Parsnip is my special friend.

Song: 'Old MacDonald had a farm. E-i-e-i-o!'

Story: 'The Three Little Pigs.'

Book: 'The Playdays Annual.'

TV programme: Playdays - the Patch stop.

The wind and the sun

adapted by Wayne Jackman

One morning, high up in the sky, the sun and the wind were having an argument about which of them was the strongest.

"Listen, Sun," said the wind. "I'm much stronger than you."

"Nonsense wind," replied the sun. "I've always been the strongest."

The wind did not agree. "Pah! Haven't you seen how people shake and shiver when I blow fast and strong?"

"Huh!" scoffed the sun. "I've seen how people sigh and cover their heads when I shine hot and long."

"Rubbish!" insisted the wind. "I'm the strongest."

"No," said the sun. "I'm the strongest."

"No, I am."

And so the argument went on.

Eventually, the sun and the wind decided to have a test.

"You see that gardener, down there?" said the wind.

"Yes," nodded the sun. "We'll test our powers against her."

"How?" quizzed the sun.

"Let's see which of us can snatch that coat away from her." The wind sounded very confident.

"Fine," said the sun. "You can go first."

37

"A foolish mistake, my friend," laughed the wind. "I'll blow that coat off her in no time. It'll be a breeze. Ha, ha, ha!"

The wind took a deep breath and began to blow.

"Whooooooooooosh!"

The sun looked on as the gardener pulled her coat tight around her. "Well, blow me," said the sun. "It didn't work."

"Pah! I was just practising. Watch this!"

The wind took an even deeper breath and then blew as hard as he could.

"Whooooooooooooooooooooooooosh!"

The gardener put down her tools and fastened her coat all the way up to her chin.

The sun teased the wind. "I thought you were strong."

"All right!" protested the wind. "Now, I'll puff harder than I have ever puffed before. Just watch me blow that coat away. Whoooooooooooooooooooooooooooooooooooooooosh!"

The wind was exhausted. "I've run out of puff," he said.

The sun smiled. "Do you give up?"

"Yes!" said the wind, still out of breath and very angry. "But, if I can't do it, neither will you."

The sun smiled and smiled. And the more the sun smiled, the warmer it became.

The gardener wiped her brow, loosened her coat and continued gardening.

"Ha!" laughed the wind. "I told you you couldn't do it."

"I'm just warming up," said the sun.

And the sun smiled a broad and happy smile. Soon it was so warm that the gardener stopped her work to undo the buttons on her coat.

The wind looked down at the gardener. "She's still wearing her coat. You haven't won."

"I haven't finished, yet," said the sun, smiling even more.

The gardener became so hot that she put down her tools, wiped her brow and took off her coat.

"You've won," said the wind, angrily.

"Of course," said the sun. "You thought you could win by huffing and puffing like a bully but I won by being gentle and warm."

The wind blew away, and he never challenged the sun again.

40

Which clothes?

Who is dressed for the sun?   Who is dressed for the rain?

Autumn Leaves

Autumn is a great time to collect leaves. When you go outside see if you can find some like these.

Sycamore These leaves make great...helicopters!

Silver Birch This tree has a silvery bark!

Oak Can you spot any acorns?

Hazel Hazelnuts are food for mice and squirrels.

When you have collected the leaves, why not:

Stick them on paper.

Copy, draw and paint them.

Dip them in paint and print them on to paper.

Put some paper on top of a leaf. Now, scribble on the paper with a pencil and see what happens!"

Letters in a Muddle

These letters have got lost.
Can you draw a line from each
letter to the right house?

A. Pink
4 Jolly Road

Mr. Black
1 Jolly Road

T. Green
5 Jolly Road

B. Orange
2 Jolly Rd.

V. Brown
3 Jolly Road

Poppy's favourite things

Food: Sardine and banana sandwiches!

Colour: Orange - like my fur.

Number: er...2, no...4, no...2.

Animal: Cats, especially lions and tigers!

Song: 'Wiggly Woo.'

Story: 'Puss-in-boots.'

Book: 'The Playdays Annual.'

TV programme: Playdays - Poppy's stop.

Pairs of Shoes

Can you match the person to their shoes?

COMPETITION

90 SUPER PRIZES TO BE WON!

30
PLAYDAYS
'LIVE ON STAGE'
CASSETTES
from BMG Kidz UK

20
GIANT FLOOR
PUZZLES

20
PICTURE CARD
GAMES

20
WOODEN
'SEE INSIDE'
JIGSAWS

Michael Stanfield toys and games are available at all major toy shops and superstores.

HOW TO ENTER

It's easy! All you have to do is answer this simple question:

At which stop would you find Mr Jolly?

Write the answer on a postcard or envelope, with your name, age and address.

Send to:
**Playdays Competition, Marketing Department, Egmont Publishing,
PO Box III, Great Ducie Street, Manchester M60 3BL.**

Closing date: 1st February 1996.

The first 90 correct entries selected at random after the closing date will win a prize.

Footprints in the Snow

Someone has made a snowman.
Follow the footprints to find out who it was.

Answer: Peggy

55

Make a Snowflake

Did you know that every flake of snow is different?
Make one with me.

You will need:

some scissors
a circle of card

Fold the paper in half..

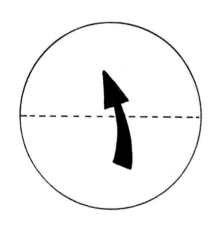

and again...

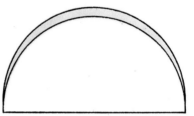

and again...

until you have a triangle.

Now, cut out little bits all around the sides.

Unfold it, very carefully.

There - a snowflake!

And there won't be another like it in
the whole world!

Jolly Snowmen

a) How many snowmen are wearing red hats and scarves?
b) How many snowmen are wearing blue hats and scarves?
c) How many snowmen are wearing green hats and scarves?
d) Point to the sad snowman.

Answers a) 4; b) 3; c) 2

58

The Wriggling Snowman

The snowman in my garden said,
Oh dear, I beg your pardon.
But every time it snows
The snowflakes tickle my toes.
The tickling makes me giggle
And when I giggle, I wriggle.
Though a snowman should stand still,
I know. The snowflakes make me wriggle so!"

Colour the snowman in.

Animal Rescue

Some of the animals have escaped from the zoo.
The Playdays friends have been asked to help find
the animals. Use a button or counter for each player
and throw a die to see how many squares to travel.
The first player to reach the zoo is the winner.

1

2

3

Traffic lights are green. Go forward one space.

4

5

6

13

12

Mr. Jolly finds a parrot. Move 2 spaces.

Why Bird finds a giraffe. Move 2 spaces.

7

11

8

10

9

Lizzie finds the elephant but he won't move. Go back 2 spaces.

Squawk

Moo! Moo!

60